Sometimes

I Wanna

Scream,

Instead

I Write.

Poems

AF235414

Magnolia D. Reeves

Sometimes I Wanna Scream, Instead I Write.

Poems

Magnolia D. Reeves

Bibliografische Information der Deutschen Nationalbibliothek:
Die Deutsche Nationalbibliothek verzeichnet diese Publikation
in der Deutschen Nationalbibliografie; detaillierte
bibliografische Daten sind im Internet über http://dnb.dnb.de
abrufbar.

Herstellung und Verlag: BoD – Books on Demand, Norderstedt

ISBN: 978-3-7543-9537-0

FOR YOU AND FOR ME,

for those who brought me pain,

for those who taught me love

and for those who made me the person

i am today.

dear reader,

if you're reading this book, you're either into poetry or going through something just the way i did. and maybe you're looking for a solution to all your problems here. truth be told: i don't have one. i don't have a solution for whatever you're struggling with. i can't heal your broken heart or glue broken pieces back together. but i can promise you that you're not alone with what you're feeling. i have been there, in a deep hole similar to yours. i've experienced it and i promise there are better days coming. never give up on the little thing called **hope.** i've been writing since i was a little child. back then i wrote christmas poems for my family each year. in second grade i wrote a poem about what friendship meant to me. it had only six lines and was as profound as a poem from an eight years old child could be. and still: writing always had some sort of healing effect on me.

i have always written to understand my surrounding and what was happening to me better. sometimes the pages in my notebook blurred through my tears. sometimes my words allowed me to relive the first moment i ever felt butterflies in my stomach. writing has been my solution to all the shit that happened it the world. every time i felt as if i was being overdramatic, i grabbed my pen and wrote an even more dramatic poem. and it always helped. poetry has been my way of coping throughout my teenage years. poetry has helped me tremendously with moving forward and growing up. and maybe my words can accompany you on your way of moving forward and growing up, no matter what age you are. each and every person is going through something. for me it was anxiety, loneliness and the feeling of never being enough. whatever it is for you, i can't heal your wounds but i can help you get through it. we've been in this together the second you reached for my book.

sincerely yours,

the author.

C H A P T E R S

ONE
THROUGH THE
DARKNESS

i am feeling lost and empty

the worst feeling in the world

worse than being sad

even worse than overthinking

hopelessness – nothing is as bad

numbness, no feelings to cling on to

drowning in the void

crying would be freeing

still, i can't seem to cry

not feeling anything

happiness is such a precious gift

not thinking twice, going for it, just doing things

my hope, my luck, my smile –

all those things are lost

i'd do anything to go back in time –

what does it cost?

i want to go back to the moment i fell

avoid the cliff and let myself grow wings

i can't even pinpoint what pushed

and pulled me down

want to be one of those happy pink glitter girls

that are in movies shown

-lost and (not) found

sometimes everything is good and right

and things still go wrong

so marvelously wrong

it takes one second, it takes not long

when everything is too much to take

and the room starts closing in

and suddenly it seems too small

i fill pages in seconds

like leaves litter the ground in fall

writing is my way of coping

the only way to calm the storm

that is raging inside my head

while sad songs fill the darkness

surrounding me, the pathetic figure in my bed

afraid to speak up, afraid to stay silent

thought a lot and overthought a lot

i could write a novel about my mind

but that would be the saddest plot

it's probably just me being dramatic though

i'm hurting, screaming but weirdly okay

because that's what i have to be

and that's just a normal average day as me

-my "pretty damn normal"

talking to somebody might help

but talking has never been a strength of mine

i'd rather pretend

and have everybody think i'm fine

i want to tell them what i'm struggling with

but i'd rather have my loved ones happy

and that's the truth even if it sounds so sappy

i can't talk to the people i love

don't want to burden them in any way

or maybe i'm just afraid that they won't stay

i hate being this problematic, this dramatic

i want to be an optimist

but that's a thing that's still on my bucket list

it's ironic: looking forward to the weekend

and still hating it, wanting it to end

days of loneliness, not knowing what to do

because there is so much

but i just don't have the strength to

people make me want to run

and lock myself away

right now, though i'd rather be nervous

than hopeless and sad

i want to leave and escape my life, my body

i look forward to the noise distracting me

to laughter and familiarity filling the room

i could really use a hug and that's okay

while looking forward

to the torturously slow coming monday

-noisy weekend void

falling for fictional characters has always been so easy

admiring friends, admiring relatives, but never admiring myself

even though they say you have to love yourself before anybody else

but i never really loved myself, never really wanted to be me

apologizing for speaking, for laughing, for feeling

because they are bored and annoyed just by me being there

because nobody enjoys talking to me, would ever do it willingly

but eventually i just wouldn't want to talk to me, that's my thing

the shadows overwhelm me whenever i think too much too long

the fear of them judging me when i'm the only one doing so

the fear of them only pretending to like me when i can't even pretend

sometimes the raging storm inside my mind is way too strong

i overthink, get too nervous to go out on some days

so many mistakes for me to make, so many things to go wrong

tiny things nobody would ever think of suddenly are huge and scary

but i can't help it so i paint my world in black and grays

-worry gives small things a big shadow

our teacher once told us that using smart words isn't the same as being smart

yet – some words make language seem like art

nobody knows what some words actually mean

they're getting read, not understood, just seen

hiding feelings behind smart words is easier than anything

because we don't look behind the curtains, don't care about understanding

make up hides many forms of pain

just like that do beautiful sounding words for sad things the same

i choose to smile and nod when asked if i am fine

the choice to be an eccedentesiast* is mine

*eccedentesiast: someone who hides pain behind a smile

i don't know who i am

feel like i don't know myself at all

when i'm shy – it's not me, it's my anxiety

when i'm confident – it's not me, it's only a damn wall

i'm trying my best to be okay

my mum thinks those are only lyrics to a song

trying not to let her see the salty drops running down my face

smiling and laughing when she walks in

because i've been doing that for way too long

-to anson seabra, whose songs have often made me cry

school project

i don't want this night to end,

don't want to see the light

i'm going to cry myself into oblivion

and hope this night will never end,

i hope it lasts forever

i'm sorry for disappointing you

over and over again

even though you don't ask for many things

i still can't seem to make you happy

i'm sorry for hurting you

over and over again

even though you're way too good for me

i still can't seem to figure out how to be what you deserve

i'm sorry for making you feel worth less than you are

over and over again

even though to me you're smart and funny and the light of every room

i still can't seem to make you feel as special as you are

i'm sorry for not being enough

over and over again

even though you deserve the best, deserve the world

i still can't seem to give you the tiniest piece of that

i'm sorry for loving you when you actually deserve the world

and that world isn't me

promises are meant to be broken

loyalty is only a social construct, a meaningless word

trust is something you should have in nobody but yourself

expectations? cross that out completely

promises – why did i believe they are meant to be kept?

when all promises just end up being lies

i keep them, set my priorities but i'm the only one

promises are meant to be broken

loyalty – no lying, cheating or betraying

it isn't that hard but why should i be loyal?

why be loyal when you can think about nobody but yourself?

loyalty is only a social construct, a meaningless word

trust – opening up the heart, letting people in

still, i always choose the wrong ones to let in

or maybe there's no right and wrong and people suck

trust is something you should have in nobody but yourself

expectations – i always told myself not to get too fond of them

but i careless and naïve because you changed me

you taught me hope and i expected you'd be the one i could trust

expectations – cross that out completely

i should've known it because it happens every god damn time

nothing lasts and nobody stays

i shouldn't trust because i'll end up getting disappointed

or maybe i'm just the disappointment

when did i go from eating carelessly

to either exercising every day or hating me?

when did i go from seeing my reflection and not feeling sorrow

to pinching my flesh, criticizing the person i see in the mirror?

when did i go from eating sweets and pizza without a second thought

to being afraid of eating in public because i feel caught?

when did i go from seeing and acknowledging my beauty

to rather being sad, depressed and moody?

when did i go from happiness

to exercising more and eating less?

well – maybe that's modern-day society

-when

life doesn't go the way we want

it never did, it never will

"but it's okay", she says

with tears running down her face

sometimes we're alone

with only ourselves, our mind and our thoughts

"but it's okay", she says

silently screaming into the void, begging for someone to hear

on some days we can only watch life pass by

watch how others are smiling, giggling, laughing

"but it's okay", she says

forgetting how to lift up the corner of her lips

jealousy is a human trait we're all familiar with

jealous of their money, their family, friends and happiness

"but it's okay", she says

even though she has none of that

"but it's okay", she says

because she's used to it

"but it's okay", she says

because she doesn't deserve it anyways

-it always is okay

sometimes i wanna scream.

instead, i write.

i don't want much

i just want to be okay

i just want the happiness to stay

for longer than ten minutes

i just want to be alright

i just don't want to cry every night

instead of sleeping, dreaming, being careless

i just want to say i'm fine and mean it

i just want my life to be a little easier, only just a little bit

is it too much to ask for?

i just don't want to try anymore

i just want everything to be like before

when i was young and blind but smiling bright

i'm tired of trying to be happy when i can't seem to be

but not only i feel that way, that's not about me

everybody wants that happiness, not much, only that

-wanted

hey google, what's the definition of happiness?

well, it's the state of being happy, happy and careless

i mean, what's there to define?

i should know myself that life is no "rise and shine"

and still "she struggled to find happiness in her life"

i'm looking at pictures of myself

a smile on my face and i can't help but feel sad

because i don't recognize the girl i'm looking at

because i don't remember happiness, the feeling

because today silent tears are straining my cheeks while staring at the ceiling

i can't remember the last time everything was fine

hey google, what am i supposed to do when my life seems to fall apart?

stay strong, it's temporary, move on, be positive, be smart

but how do you move on when all you see is black?

i can't seem to grasp onto the light, no going forward – only back

i'm lost, i'm out of control

i'm not living, doing nothing but existing

i want to be okay, just want to be alright

but i am not and who knows if i'll not cry every night

life will be fine one day – even if i'm not today

i lost hope, i don't think happiness will ever stay

but maybe i'll just google it

-my google search history

i don't hate my life, am not tired of it yet

but tired of existing, existing until nothings makes sense anymore

a steep ascent - only to pause at the top, then collapse, deeper than before

hitting rock bottom, falling into the big "sad"

i want to live but not in pain, in sadness and in grief

but tears don't stop, smiling hurts

can sad thoughts ever turn into happy words?

even though it's my voice, my story and i'm the editor in chief

-author of my story

today is one of those quietly staring at the wall kind of days

hours just passing by in the slowest pace

counting the minutes until i can finally go to bed

without my mum suspecting that i'm feeling sad

which i'm not - just empty and tired, maybe a little indifferent

and those scars will always stay, they can't be mend

today is one of those not wanting to get up kind of days

because it costs so much strength and for something that simple there is no praise

dullness in the air, inside out a storm is raging

and i'm too numb for smiling, caring, for engaging

sometimes a day just can't be a good one

all alone, with my hopes and dreams and happiness just gone

today is one of those kind of days

they come and go, come back again

but not a single one stays

right now, i hate myself, my body, my life and my mind

and maybe i'll feel the same tomorrow

maybe tomorrow is another day of that kind

but i'll survive

those kind of days

-one of those days

i think i grew up too fast

i think i'm too mature for my age

i think too much

when others my age just don't

to me the world is ending

when others my age are going to party

to me the people i love matter more than anything

when others my age only care about fun

to me it is scary to go outside

when others my age don't want to come inside

to me the things i want are less important

when others my age just do their thing

to me caring too much is normal

when others my age only ever act careless

i think i don't understand everybody acting like a child

i think i grew up too fast to understand

or maybe this isn't the right way to say it

maybe it's rather that life broke me too early

now i don't know anymore

how to breathe

with all this anxiety here choking me

-metamorphosis

it's been a long day of not feeling enough

because even at the things i'm the best

somebody will always be better

many more days of doubting my worth

are yet to come

because i'll never be enough

i don't feel pain

because i do not differ

between feeling

and being

pain is a part of me

i'm not in pain

i am the pain

the pain is me

through every street

around every corner

we go hand in hand

it stings

it hurts

it aches

but in the end, i don't differ

between feeling pain

and forcing my lungs to breathe

because i'm used to both

it's what i've been doing

since i've been born

-pain inside of me

life's s test

and i'm someone who studies

life is teaching lessons

continuously and every day

but as many notes

as i take

i can't seem to keep them

inside my tiny little brain

sadly

life isn't about studying

it's "just doing, just being, just living"

in the moment events occur

i have always been

someone who studies

to pass the test

i give everything i have

all i am

and now

i'm failing life

-study session

and if they asked

"what's going on in your life right now?"

i'd laugh

through a tear clouded

dazed and blurry vision

"too much"

i'd say,

"i can't even put it in words"

i'd say,

and then i'd tell them anyways

and pour my soul into their cup

up until the rim

and even overflowing

the words replayed before

a thousand times already

inside my mind only

because yes, it is too much

but no, it's not that i can't put it in words

i can - i have the words neatly sorted out

calling all the demons by their names

but they don't ask

nobody ever really asks

and my glass is always overflowing

-overflowing

it really shouldn't matter

that you forgot my name

because it really doesn't matter

but actually

to me, it matters

because you just confirmed

what i've been thinking all day long

that i'm not enough

and that i'll never be

you just confirmed

that i'm invisible

that i don't exist

but it really doesn't matter

i thank you from the bottom of my heart

for forgetting this name of mine

when i already wasn't feeling fine

because you confirmed today

that i don't matter anyway

-thanking my english teacher

today it feels as if

i hate the things

i love the most

you make me hate

the things i love the most

and more than that

you make me hate myself

even though i'm not

one of the things i love

-love to hate

i wouldn't say that i'm depressed

i also wouldn't say i'm stressed

i just got used to not feeling content

i'm unhappy as if it was a commitment

it's not that i've always been sad

it's not that i've always felt bad

but for too long periods of time, i guess

i haven't felt a glimpse of happiness

you feel happy once again

no matter where or when

the highest highs, the brightest days

always followed by darkness anyways

feeling happy again gets more complicated

once that temporary happiness is faded

and replaced by numbness and indifference

no pinkish-red glasses, black n' white lens

a day on cloud seven

a day in heaven

is always followed by a broken shell

a day in hell

happiness is horror because it never stays

passes by as if it had to win a race

i'd rather live in sorrow

than feel happy today and numb tomorrow

when i'm happy i wait for the sadness

when i'm sad i miss the happiness

they both come hand in hand

it's a vicious cycle without end

-happy and sad

for the first time in forever

today, we were together

something so very ordinary

something so very necessary

something we haven't been

in almost an eternity

it's like i forgot what it felt like

and it hit me while bowling with my life

hit me like a strike

suddenly the blooming

fresh air

messy hair

rainbow sparkling unicorns

roses without thorns -

kinda feeling hit me in the face

softened my smile, softened my gaze

and i remembered

the feeling of happiness

and i realized

how i much i've had that feeling missed

everything was once again okay

but from normal and alright we're far away

a moment the world seemed to be fine

and everything felt normal for only a short time

the world was healed, the scars mended

the tears subsided, the pain ended

but reality came crushing down

being together isn't allowed

i wanna scream, i wanna shout

i wanna break out

can't cope with loneliness and distance anymore

want things to be as they were before

but they will never be

my eyes dried out from all the tears

my heart bleed out from all the wounds

my youth is over

and when it asks, i'll tell my child

"no, my dear, my youth wasn't crazy or wild

i spent all my time alone, crying in my room,

facetime, skype, whatsapp and zoom"

and i'll hope that if my child one day asks

it doesn't have to wear those fucking face masks

-covid19

i just wanna be appreciated

by myself

more than anyone else

usually, write to people that are existing

but all you are is being missing

though i won't hang up a 'missing'-poster at the mall

because i don't know who you are at all

what you look like,

if you rather walk or go by bike,

what you dream of at night,

what makes your smile shine bright,

if you read the same books as me,

if you prefer coffee or tea

i don't know you if i'm being honest

but you're the reason there's a hole inside my chest

i'd say you left me

but you didn't

you were never here in the first place

there always was that taunting empty space

and only you can fill that void

but then again – you can't, you won't

you don't know who i am

you don't give a damn

you don't care

you are not there and that's okay

if i was you, i wouldn't stay -

just like everybody else who walked away

and i don't blame them at all

i wish i had three wishes

i wish i was like them

wild and bold and beautiful

strong and fierce and confident

i wish i had three wishes

i wish i wasn't me

shy and quiet and nerdy

anxious and weak and whiny

i wish i had three wishes

i wish i would belong

no loneliness and emptiness and silence

no self-hatred and anxiety and tears

i wish i had more than three wishes

i wish the pain would stop

i wish i could disappear

i wish i wouldn't exist at all

i wish…

-genie in a bottle

there is this monster

inside my head

untamable

immutable

invincible

sometimes

often

the monster breaks out

it screeches and screams

it whines and grunts

claws digging into my flesh

teeth piercing through my skin

and before it eats me up

inside out

i turn around

and run

i run and run

and never turn back

and then

only in domestic solitude

the monster calms down

the noises subsiding

falling asleep

charging

to once again

on another day soon

hunt me

choke me

rip me apart

and one day

the monster inside my head

will break me

will kill me

as if i wasn't broken before

as if i wasn't dead before

once and for all

social anxiety

TWO

NEVER SAID

OUT LOUD

things were easier not long a

now "not long ago" seems far away

we used to laugh and joke about the future

the utopian dream is faded though

i have known you when your eyes seemed to be a little brighter

and your smile forced a little less

i miss the times we'd spend talking for hours

when you didn't have to be a fighter

we've been through so much together

seen you bleeding and lying on the floor

you've seen me cry then cry a little more

we swore we'd be for always and forever

but things took a turn

life isn't about secrets and laughter anymore

it's worrying about way too many things

wondering if the forest will ever stop to burn

both our demons seem to drag us apart

further than any distance ever could

i've loved you before i even know i did

no matter what you're still inside my heart

you deserve the destiny to be more kind

deserve so much more, a much better life

i don't want to need to worry day and night

and still, i can't keep you out of my mind

drowning in the thought of you not being here

you said i do not need to worry

you said you wouldn't end it yet

but of course, i worry and live in fear

-angel

i realized i never wrote about you

rarely even thought about you lately

because i tried to forget that you exist

because i wanted to shut the pain you brought me out

because the silence of your absence is too loud

i realized a long time ago that i don't need you anymore

the little me would have but you weren't there

i would have loved to play with you more often

would have loved to hear you say "i love you more" one more time

i would love to never see you again

i realized that no matter what i can't hate you

and yet i hate the way you look the way you

i hear you screaming at my mum

i smell the alcohol on your breath and see the blood shot eyes

i think of all the broken promises and lies

i realized i can't think of you as the person you were supposed to be

i try to think of moments in which you cared enough

came up with me crying, you screaming at me

came up with you telling me you did it me you didn't even want me

came up with none of the "dad is my superhero" bullshit i should see

-dad is not my superhero

bling – you've got a new message

just in case you decide

to ever get your shit together

just wanted to let you know

that it's too late

adults are supposed to answer all the questions

to teach, to nurture, to decide

adults are supposed to make decisions

to be smart and right and mature

but in the end being an adult makes no sense

little infants fight, throw insults and toys

because they don't know better

it's not their job to do to right thing, to be mature

because they don't need to be adults just yet

and they'll stop fighting once they hear their parents raised voice

adults fight, throw insults and make a mess

too frustrated to care

it's their job to do the right thing, it's their job to be mature

they should be adults but they are not

they should make decisions for their own happiness

happiness is not a given, that much i know

we aspire to be happy but do nothing for it

instead of fighting we press "pause" and stay where we are

change means being lost, change is scary

because we are afraid of new beginnings – so we choose sorrow?

the first step of new beginnings are the little things

cut off what's not good for you

throw out what drags you down

let go of what holds you back

butterflies can't fly with broken wings

we shorten our own wings day to day

with choosing not to spread them we forget how to fly

but flying means happiness and freedom

and what's life without that?

let's grow ourselves wings and fly and be

-let's fly

i can't make you love me

or even like me

but how can i

make you notice me?

only for a moment

you talk about your brother
and you say he has it all
when he's still living with his mother
doing nothing, no job, no family
observing life from afar,
observing from behind a wall

you talk about todays' society
and you say there are only three classes
when there's so much more variety
not only black and white but gray and colors
not only rich and poor, perfection and mess

you talk about not being content
and you say you'll never be
when you could easily rethink the way your life is spend
it's your own fault you're this desperate
it's your own fault you missed the chance, that you don't see

you talk about your mobile game
and you say things i don't hear because i stop listening
it really doesn't matter, it's always the same
empty words, no meaning, no connection
empty words just said to say anything

you talk and never seem to stop, you talk

and you say things i'll never agree with

when i would like to jump out of the window, just go on a walk

wishing to be anywhere except with you is reality

being close to you, willingly talking to you seems like an ancient myth

-what it feels like to be alone in a car with you

"why?" is such a big thing to ask someone

because there is no answer, no wrong or right

or rather there are way too many

still there is the same "why" i ask myself at night

why do people feel the need to turn to alcohol? why?

to let loose, to party, to have fun?

to drown sorrow, doubts and grief?

because you are tired of living but not tired enough to never see the sun?

or is it because you just can't help it?

because you've been drowning for way too long

and everybody gave up on trying to get up from under the surface

because you're too far from the shallow now, just like in the song?

you can try to save a drowning sailor

but at some point, there is no chance of coming back up again

so, you stop, stop asking "why?", stop trying

you let go of that hopelessly drowning man

-the ship has sailed

"i'm happy we've talked about this.", you told me

smiles and "i love you's" were being shared

you told me to have fun, to text you and be nice

then i got out of the car and you turned the ignition key

we didn't really talk about this

you just go on and pretend our conversation changed the world

in reality you just don't want to hear your daughter say it out loud

you know the truth but can't admit it and bid me a goodbye with a kiss

we were sitting in a car, the silence filled with our sniffing sound

because life is not fair and it never will be

but life is also not hopeless and you're an adult

you should know that and tell me that, not the other way around

you see the prizes rise and the money melt in your hands

the concert of your favorite artist is called off

shopping with mask, cinemas are closed and your husband is a bitch

and life sucks but mum, it's fine – hope isn't cancelled

hope isn't cancelled and love isn't cancelled

and even though sadness, grief and anger are the only thing you feel right now

you should smile and laugh and be happy you're alive

you're alive and i hope you haven't forgotten how that felt

-oh, mum

have you asked yourself where things went wrong?

and when?

when did life hit you and begin to haunt you?

when did the sweet and innocent part of you just vanish?

have you ever wanted to go back in time?

and experience the joy of being a child again?

-asking a notebook questions it won't answer because it's just paper with ink on it

1,2,3: drink – it's so much fun

4,5,6: where am i? who are you? what's up?

7,8,9: hey stranger! where are we going?

stutter – no clear sentence

1,2,3: drink - it's so much fun

4,5,6: blackout, memory gone, shoving aspirin down my throat

7,8,9: what happened? how did i get home?

many questions but no answer

1,2,3: drink – it's so much fun

4,5,6: next day, next week, next month - when is it ever gonna stop?

7,8,9: repeat, more, more – always

who even am i?

1,2,3: drink – it's so much fun

4,5,6: it's never gonna stop, giving up on myself

7, 8,9: messy hair, deadly pale skin, empty eyes

that's me

1,2,3: drink – it's so much fun

4,5,6: losing, losing, losing myself

7,8,9: too much, too late, no take back

completely lost

your smile beams brighter than the sun

your smile lights up every room you enter

but your smile isn't all too special

because you gift it to everyone who crosses your way

you have a heart made out of gold

you're sweet and kind and pure and nice

but your kindness isn't all too special

because everyone you meet sees you that way

you say you trust me with your whole heart

you talk to me about anything and everything

but your trust in me isn't all too special

because everyone seems to know you the same amount i do

you say you care and that you need me

you say those things and still don't call or text

but that's okay

because i never even expected you to

you tell me that i am your best friend

you always tell me that and never show it

but that's okay

because everybody feels like they are your best friend

you tell others that i'm your friend

you never introduce me as your best friend

but that's okay

because maybe a friend is all i am to you

you are my best friend – but am i yours?

see you again

we haven't seen each other in mere months

we haven't talked in a few weeks

we haven't even texted in over seven days

and i want to see you again

and hold you close

to know you're save

for only a short moment

one day

before it is too late

i don't know you the longest

or the best

and neither am i always here for you

but you mean the world to me

it hurts

to see what you've become

but it doesn't hurt as much

as it used to

because i let you go

forever

my father's point of view:

behind my back the door slams shut

the hollow room filled with an echoing thud

i look but there's nothing around

i listen but i hear no other sound

the void filling me, taunting me

a room full of emptiness is all i see

the room seems to mirror what i feel

lost control of the steering wheel

it's only me now-days

everybody has chosen different ways

it's only me and the deafening silence

no hand to hold, no guidance

there's no radio music to blast

the voices in my head take over at last

not even whistling can ease the pain

no way 'round admitting i went insane

the first time the door behind me fell shut

the room was filled with the same echoing thud

on the spot the floor turned into a dark hole

and darkness swallowed me whole

suddenly i had time to realize

time to open my eyes

too much time spent inside my head

too much time spent wishing i was dead

and after all i came to a conclusion

after delusion and confusion

there's nobody else to blame

and now i allow myself the walk of shame

i was in the wrong

it was my fault all along -

who's the source of all my problems, mirror on the wall?

staring back at me is my own face after all

but that is only poetry

and he will never see

he will never see his reflection

and nothing but perfection

when asking the mirror whom to blame

it's always us, always the same

-your fault

what would i give to hear your voice one last time?

because every time i enter the door

i hear you

the snoring while slowly tapping

to the bathroom at night

what would i give to see your face one last time?

because i forgot

what you looked like

the color of your eyes i wouldn't even know

the shape of you face became a stranger to me

what would i give to relive our moments one last time?

because i can't remember them at all

i was too young

i can't remember what your hugs felt like

i can't remember and i'm afraid i will forget you

what would i give to say goodbye one last time?

because i wish i told you i loved you

and hugged you real tight

i didn't know i would never have to chance for it again

i just told you i'd see you tomorrow but i never did

what would i give to go back in time?

because it's been five years

and i'm only allowing myself to write you now

time is supposed to heal all wounds

but here i am - crying because the ones you left never will

what would i give to know what you think of me today?

because i hope you'd be proud

i hope i'd make you proud

i wish you would tell me i'm enough, that i'll figure it out

but i will never hear you say you love me ever again

-i miss you

i always wanted you

to be like you

to be with you

i always wanted you to like me back

to cherish me the same way i do

to even love me to same way i do

i always wanted us to have a "forever"

to need each other

to be together

i always wanted you to be mine

and in some way, i thought you were

but you never wanted me back

i always wanted to have a place inside your heart

but i have been replaced

even though the place was never mine

i always thought you'd be the one to stay

but you didn't

but you then you left me behind, left as if i never mattered

i never thought you'd break my heart

because this isn't a love story and not about heart break

but friends can break your heart too

-heartbreak

you don't want to understand

that between us there is no relationship to be mend

you were never present

now your presence is just really unpleasant

you were never good at your job as a dad

you were a father but never a parent isn't that sad?

you chose to leave your children high and dry

all you do is try, lie and deny

you left me alone but never left my sight

when i see you all i can feel is despite

you ask and ask and ask question all day long

but your voice just sounds so terribly wrong

you've always lived in the same house as i do

and still, i try everything not to see you

you know our family has always been twisted

now days i try to pretend you never even existed

after all i never held you all too dear

because years ago you chose over us - your beer

-an alcoholic parent does not exist

there's this darkness inside of me

sometimes it takes over

overshadowing all that's good

and i want you to be sorry

when i'm the one who's wrong

i want you to feel guilt

to be in pain

to see your tears flow down your cheeks

i want to torture you

i want you to suffer

and i know how wrong that is

how sick that is

my mind yells at me

to stop, to stop, to do nothing but stop

but i don't

i want you to suffer

more than i do

only then do i feel better

only then did i reach my goal

breaking you means success to me

-her words

i still talk to you

every single night

you don't ask about my day

and you never answer

but i know you're with me

every step of the way

i know you're listening

and that you'd complain

about everything and anything

if you were here

but really, you're not

you're not here anymore

and still, i will admit

the conversations i have with you

are the best i have all day

-my mum's perspective

i let you go

so i could grow,

finally grow out of you

and so did you, too

i let you go

so i could move on

finally move on from you

and so did you, too

i let you go

so i could forget

finally forget about you

and so did you, too

it hurt to let you go

not for a long time though

i wish it hurt more

i wish it meant more

i wish it broke me at least a little

but there was no heartbreak,

no heartache

it just was over, gone, passed

and at last

letting go of you

was the best thing i could do

our past doesn't matter

the way it is today – it's better

-no regret

say what you think

but think about what you say

holding a drink in my hand

sipping on a cocktail glass

i don't think it will ever feel normal

seeing other people drink

hearing their raised voices

i don't think it will ever not remind me of you

when voices get louder

when a drink turns into five or six or seven

i can't help but see your face in front of me

as if it wasn't enough you stole my childhood

as if it wasn't enough stole my smile

as if it wasn't enough you stole my hope

you had to take my teenage years too

you had to take my adulthood too

you had to take everything from me

just one sip, one glass, one bottle

just another ruined life

-party nights

i guess you'll never know

that i am really sorry

i wasn't there

i wasn't fair

i acted as if i didn't care

deep down i thought you wouldn't mind

and i was so blind

wish i could rewind

i guess i never knew

that i mattered to you

i actually just found out yesterday

and our story ended years back from today

now i think of all the things i would say

but we haven't talked in forever

and we probably won't talk again ever

i never wanted to hurt you, never

i guess i'll know from now on

that i was the worst possible friend to you

you were family

you meant the world to me

and i never meant to be

the person that let you down like that

cause i thought you didn't need me

the person that replaced you like that

cause i thought you replaced me

the person that lost you like that

cause i didn't want to lose you

i guess you might hate me

i guess you don't care anymore

about what i said

or what i say

but i hope you're doing okay

and going your way

and that you'll forgive me one day

and maybe

in another world

our friendship didn't have to end

because i was a better best friend

but here

in this world

i'm sorry

in this world

i wonder if you ever think about me too

in this world

i wonder if you kept the necklace

because in my heart and room it still has a place

and i guess you'll never know

-mona lisa

and one day,

far from, today,

far from tomorrow,

if only in a different world,

if only in a different universe,

things might be different,

things might be alright.

and maybe, just maybe –

we could be a family.

but not in this reality.

in this reality,

we are broken.

and no glue can fix

what never was whole.

and still there is this hole.

a hole shaped like us –

what we could have been,

what we were supposed to be.

and it will never get filled –

because nothing of "us" is left.

-family

THREE
CONQUERING
THE WORLD

i write myself a whole new world

i dive right into it

i live in it

i fall in love with it

the real world i shut out

and forget about the existence of her

because she often sucks

waiting is the shadow that haunts you day to day

and life is like a waiting room

living is like being in there as a child

constantly waiting for anything and everything

being bound to the known and waiting to be wild

always waiting for something to happen

waiting to get called in by the doctor

to finally go home and play and laugh and live

but there will always be a doctor before

and you're waiting to escape that world – known, cold and stiff

never wanting to leave that sterile plastic seat

something bad might happen

the sharp needle of the syringe waiting to pierce your skin

the smell of cleanness eating you up inside out

the doctor smiling exaggeratedly and grabbing your chin

it's an endless back and forth

a never-ending cycle

waiting for a change of scenery

while hoping to stay just where you are

hoping to stay just where you are

because uncertainty is scaring you just as much as it is scaring me

-waiting room thoughts

i've always liked the fall

when leaves turn golden

and the whole world seems to burn

when everything is fine and without any trace of concern

it's ironic how fall seems to give me hope

when it's actually the beginning of the end

when the world is actually losing its last splash of color with the last fallen leaf

in the blink of an eye, in a moment so brief

foggy mornings, rainy noon and icy night

the trees have shed their coats

while we put ours on paired with scarf and mittens

crunching leaves accompanying our very steps like purring kittens

when only black and white and gray are left

i'm always feeling hopeful

because it's not different than the year before and the year bevor that year

it reminds me that change is not to fear

the deadly winter is always followed by the blossoming of tiny buds

it never stays that hollow, stays that dark

endings don't mean there won't be new beginnings

hot cocoa in one hand, waiting for the always coming springs

-the hope of fall

people are crying

people are dying

people are trying

trying to live, to love, to laugh

flowers are blossoming and trees are turning green

spring is coming in full force, that's what i mean

because spring doesn't know

spring comes every year again, takes away the sadness

swallows all the cold and darkness

spring is my definition of hope, of leaving behind all mess

this year it's all different though, we're still hurting, still in the dark

and still: the world is continuing to turn, following her fate

days and nights go by and people forget the date

because they still try - isn't it already too late?

but spring? he doesn't know

the skies and the seas have never been clearer

the sun has never shone brighter

the colors of the flowers have never looked prettier

and it's all because spring doesn't know

it's like somebody turned on a light

and if you look out of the window

doesn't it feel right?

things aren't that different deep inside

and maybe spring knows and just doesn't give a fuck

-spring doesn't know

crown

jewels sparkle

worn by royalty

a symbol of power

childhood dream

"shake the old man's hand, kid"
says my mum, iit's what i raised you to do"
"give your grandma a kiss, my dear"
says the older woman herself "show some kindness"

"it's what i aised you to do"
"show some kindness"
shake hands, hug, kiss, repeat, always
kindness – there is no other way for that to be expressed

they teach you to smile, bright, always
you'll seem more open, more approachable
people will like you, will only like you if you smile –
but what if all if all these things wouldn't be an option anymore?

you don't need to hug or kiss or even see a smile to be nice –
sometimes your eyes say it all
more than a thousand words will ever do
they say your eyes are the window to your soul

we can put on a mask, play hide and seek with our emotions
but even a mask can't hide our true colors
truer than all the words in the world
truer than a true loves kiss
the ones inside our eyes
-for art class

look up at the sky, my dear

a sky so blue and clear, white spots like sheep all over

look up – what do you see?

a whole new world made out of cotton candy

a kingdom fully created by yourself

fully reigned by yourself and still so incredibly fragile

one change, the wind direction, a small breeze

and the castle falls, the royal horses turn to dust, a wave swallows the tiny sheep

nothing of the kingdom you build in your mind is left

clouds made of dreams and wishes and desires

and they might stay unfulfilled

because winds change and the weather changes

and sometimes sun breaks through and sometimes no blue is left

clouds made of sorrow, anger, hate and grief

and they might be more present on some days

and building and reigning a kingdom seems impossible

and sometimes you want to give up and sometimes there's hope

clouds are made of what you want them to be made of

winds change and shapes of clouds do too

but there are always clouds to build a castle with

because clouds are not dreams or sorrow,

they are nothing but water and dust

today i felt beautiful
i looked into the mirror
with red and glassy eyes after i cried
and i felt beautiful

today i felt beautiful
i saw the pain inside my eyes
and knew i was damaged but not broken
and i felt beautiful

today i felt beautiful
because i realized that everybody hurts
and that i'm not that different
and i felt beautiful

today i felt beautiful
because i realized that everybody is
and that everybody is uniquely the same
and i felt beautiful

today i felt beautiful
because i am
and you are too
and we should all feel beautiful
tomorrow too
-beauty in the mirror

live life the way

you scroll through instagram –

continuously,

daily,

with interest

and to the fullest

even when it seems pointless

nothing lasts forever,

nothing

except hope maybe,

the little thing called hope

and sometimes hope is everything you need

to live

to exist

or just to stay alive

what do you wanna be one day?
that's an easy question, i say.
a princess, like cinderella and belle,
like elsa, like arielle.
dozens of sparkling robes in pink and blue,
owning a golden palace and my own zoo.
and i almost became a princess.
but i was only four,
and i trusted in my non existing knight in shining armour.
i believed in fairytales
and learned only much later not to trust fictional males.

what do you wanna be?
same topic, you see?
being an actress is my wish.
but i'm too shy and quiet and kind of foolish.
flashlight-thunderstorms aren't really my thing
i can't dance, act or sing.
so naturally, in the end -
fait had something different planned.
but i was only ten
and a huge movie fan.

what job do you....

i'll interrupt you here cause i know what you'll do:
what do you wanna become?
what do i wanna become?
i wanna be a teacher in elementary
a kind one, gracious, punctual and that's all that is necessary.
that's answer enough for you.
but i was only twelve…
and whether i'm blaming only maths or school in general
i bid my teacher-dream quickly farewell.
way too much yelling and bureaucracy
to be frank, that doesn't fit me

what i want to be?
no need to question me today
i don't have an answer anyway
i don't know, to be fully honest
and society makes me believe i am a lost case -
failure written in my face
but i am only thirteen,
i have no experience, have nothing seen -
how am i supposed to understand the world?
of course i mean -
i'm old enough, "already" thirteen
plan a to z have to be complete,
other wise i'm dead meat and
i'll have to concede to defeat
i need a job that is well paid,
i need some food on my plate,
i need to think ahead a full decade
damn it, no: maybe all of that can wait!

i don't understand the world, years later

my unknowingness a traitor
and now? what now?
what do i wanna become now anyway?
higher, further, more is what i dream of today
today i want way too much way too badly
but my dreams are utopical, sadly.

what do i wanna be?
what - what - what?
and never "who"
who do you want to be?
who i want to be?
"who" doesn't matter,
wrong or right, worse or better
what grade, how many points have you?
there's no,,you do you",
you do what others expect.

and i'm scared,
scared to fail,
scared not to be enough,
scared to lose myself
in an ocean of numbers
90-60-90, pretty symmetrical face -
everything else is out of place.
social media made me think,
i could live from grapes and the one or other drink,
all they do is steal my life
and take my happiness away
but believe me when i say:
none of it matters at the end of the day.
trying to keep up with the kardashians,

make-up, expensive dresses, newest vans.
no money on my bank account left behind
sick in our mind
nobody knows how to be kind
we don't laugh because we want to
but because others demand so
i can't be myself in this place,
for individuality is no space.
listen to me spill the tea:
imagine someone asked who you want to be
sounds nice - doesn't it?
but nobody asks, nobody cares.

grades matter, points matter,
no graduation and all dreams will shatter.
the number on your pay check is of importance
is she not high enough, you don't get a chance -
numbers everywhere you look
and i never understood my mathsbook
i always wondered where i'd need functions and equations in real life
i realised it ain't a deep dive
cause i can't flee -
numbers of all kinds are all i see
likes, pounds, dollar-signs, bling-bling,
numbers - that is our thing!
someone might ask
one day, who i want to become?
and i won't remember.
i lost myself in the number gibberish
while adapting and trying to fit in i vanish
i forgot who i am and who want to be
because we're always competing
there's always a race we need to be completing
clothing size, wrestling, multiple choice

don't bother with "stand up, stand tall, raise your voice"
stay invisible, quiet and small
but what if that's not who i want to be after all?

in maths class
i got lost amidst the numbers every time -
so now, i'll throw them out of the window,
without regret or sorrow.
what i want to be one day?
author of my own story-
who i want to be one day?
i don't know yet -
but my book is far from finished
why should my range of choices be diminished?
you may ask again another time though
who i want to be…
now go on and ask what i want to be
you've been waiting to question me
and i promise, i have an answer today:
i know i want to write
my own story, black on white
i can be who want to be -
a princess in a castle if that's the real me
looking back at my childish dream wish with laughter
i realise i'm living my personal happily-ever-after
i created my own fairytale
by not counting money anymore or steeping on a scale
cause i am not a number
-random number generator

teen drama, sit com, romance novel turned blockbuster
girls: giggling, laughing, screaming, pillow fights

girls: gossip, face masks, binging that new show

girls: shopping, starbucks, make-up, selfie-click

girls, girls, girls: best friends forever

real life, real world, reality is different isn't it?

it's still girls: giggling, laughing, screaming, pillow fights

it's still girls: gossip, face masks, binging that new show

it's still girls: shopping, starbucks, make-up, selfie-click

girls, girls, girls: best friends forever

the only difference is time -

forever

but even forever has an expiration date

and maybe forever ends today

or maybe there was never a forever,

never a best friend forever

girls, girls, girls: no best friend for me

-best friends forever and ever and ever

my wall is covered in photographs

tiny faces on paper pieces

framed – but not to keep them in place

framed – to conserve, to remember, to keep

to remember long passed moments

the bbqs and games on summer days

the last time we went shopping

the festival last september, one year ago by now

my wall is covered in photographs

and i wish they could move and open up

for me to climb in to relive those happy days

and actually, my wall isn't covered in photographs

my wall is covered in memories

in happiness

-snapshot

our continuously changing world

changing since the concept of time is known

 and even before that

and even though everything does, this isn't changing soon

then why is change that scary?

today is already different from yesterday

and the world is still turning

even when she seems to halt

still turning, still changing, still continuing to move

and so are we and so are our lives

why are we acting as if time has stopped?

why are we stilling our in movements, stop turning?

why press "pause" when there's a button for "play"?

-buttons

let's agree that life is everything but fair
you're so far away 6 feet and more
even though i wish you were there

let's agree that the world is a dark place
the floor gets ripped out under our feet
makes us feel uprooted, like floating through space

let's agree that tears mean actually escaping
without you near me nothing else makes sense
crying until numbness is actually a thing

let's agree that sometimes there's no hope
darkness all around you and no way out
only one person that can help you cope

let's agree that i need you more than anything right now
but you're so far away, 6 feet and more
-global pandemic

sometimes a mum only wants to be hugged really tight

but don't we do that all?

sometimes a mum only wants a short "i love you"

but don't we do that all?

sometimes a mum only wants to be needed

but don't we do that all?

sometimes a mum only wants someone to be proud of them

but don't we do that all?

sometimes a mum only wants to know that she is not alone

but don't we do that all?

sometimes a mum wants to be only human

but don't we want that all?

-we are all mums

you see her walking down the dark street

that's where all forbidden lovers meet

a girl: short skirt, high heels

you wonder, would love to know how she feels

you would love to feel her hot breath on your skin

you would love to wrap your hands around her waist, fragile and thin

you go for it, grab her, push her up against a wall, her skirt riding up

you're pushing her in the alley behind that dark club

and she's fighting, crying, screaming, her lip bleeding

but you're holding her, pressed against you, that poor thing

she screams no, she begs you to stop and you hear it

but for you it's just a sassy girl with a cute wit

she says no but her clothes say yes – or don't they?

no, she says no

and no means no

and no piece of clothing makes the acting like a piece of shit okay

-me too

a heart, living, red flesh, whole

pumping blood, pumping life through my veins

keeping me alive, that's what it does, it beats

and they walk in and act like they own it

stabbing through the thickest flesh, screaming in agony

ripping muscles apart, screaming through the tears

breaking veins into pieces, screaming against the pain

the wounds will heal, the pain will leave or not?

sadness will turn into numbness, all sewn up

wounds will heal, the scars will stay, the pain – it stays-

they leave but the pain, it stays

this is the pain of a broken heart

but not about falling in or out of love, not a love story at all

it's a story about friendship,

about them, who walked in and ripped my heart apart

they ripped me apart

-heartbreak

angel

golden shimmery

wings to fly

sent from heaven above

guardian

they tell us to "live, laugh, love"

heads up, smile, be happy

but they will never understand

how it hurts to force a smile

my life is a puzzle

a puzzle and my nemesis

puzzle pieces missing

puzzle pieces all over the place

under the table, in the wrong space

struggling to find the right fitting pieces

losing puzzle pieces through the years

pieces scattered everywhere

shuffled, swiped under the couch

forgotten in the dust, forever lost

my life is a puzzle

and it will never be complete

my life is a puzzle

and the pieces are falling apart

-jigsaw

sometimes

the noises become deafening

sometimes

the noises turn into a soft hum

and either way

i won't get used to it

my ears are ringing

and i can not escape

from all the noise

from all the silence

-paradox of the silent noise

this year it seems as if

we're standing in the never ending rain

waiting desperately, in vain

for the never coming spring awakening

for the muted birds to sing

for the butterflies to spread their wing

fruitless the tree,

fruitless the hope inside of me

hope cut down to the bone

only a greyish tint left, him and i alone

every spark of cheer replaced with despair

gone in the wind, vanished into thin air

sometimes i see the sun peaking through

sometimes i think the sky might turn blue

but no - spring drowned in oceans of sorrow

even spring, the always hopeful tomorrow

not even spring can break through the wall

not even him, nobody at all

last year i thought spring didn't give a fuck

but last year i also believed in hope and luck

those rose colored glasses broke

everything seems like nothing but a bad joke

rather than joking i feel like sleeping today

don't wake me once i dreamt myself away

wishing for it to be nothing but a nightmare

because this can't be real, this isn't fair

pinch me and tell me this is a dream

let me out of this grand scheme

rescue me out of this iron cage

wake me once spring is performing on stage

this year it seems as if

we're resigning, not trying anymore

there is no 'soon it will be over' like before

people are crying, people are dying

and spring is sighing

we're tired and spring is tired too

but once again he has to pull through

and force a smile onto our face anew

so no, hope isn't fully dead -

it's just still laying in its' winter bed

-winter hibernation

in some ways

we're all like our smartphones

slowly dying

while being used

slowly breaking

while being thrown on the ground

except we're not in a hurry

 to go grab the charger

except that once the battery is dead

here is no reboot or second chance

-zero percent

things aren't scary

until you name them

and manifest them just like that

naming things equals creating monsters

sometimes you breeze past me

not casting me a single look

sometimes i see you from afar

not knowing i still notice you

and i wonder

if you sometimes think about me

and ask yourself the same thing i do

i wonder if you ever asked yourself

if something broke me, too

the same way it did break you

words of massive destruction

language - the most beautiful thing in the world

how could it ever really hurt someone?

nobody would think of words as a weapon of massive destruction

language really is the most harmful thing in the world

not words themselves choose to destroy

it's us who give them the fuel

it's us who give them the power to destroy

words can cause no harm

while us humans might just be the embodiment of pain

-poetry analysis

"i'm scared, mommy" she said

"there are monsters under my bed"

but mommy only said "no need to be afraid, my love

no monsters here, not left or right, not below, and not above"

"i'm scared, mommy" she said again the next day

with tears in her eyes she begged mommy to stay

but mommy only said "you're a big girl. you are brave"

and the girl was laying awake for hours not feeling safe

years later she's laying awake again, sobbing, hugging her knees

"i'm scared, mum" she says but nobody is there to hear her pleas

just like years ago there are monsters under her bed

except today the monsters are more so in her head

-monsters

you remember those girls

you've seen in movies?

the underage drinking girls

illuminated with pink neon lights

colored streaks in their wild and wavy hair

glitter on their lids

lips so plump and full from kissing their best friend

moving their bodies with easy lightness to the beat

followed by old mens hungry eyes

but they? they couldn't care less

they laugh

and their laughter fills the club

once you were a little girl

you remember those dreams

of your youth being exactly like that?

you remember how you wished to be

like those girls you've seen in movies?

your youth is now

and you are nothing like the movie girls

i blink and honestly my youth is almost over

and i haven't been drunk once

haven't danced my feet deaf once

haven't kissed my best friend once

haven't catfished an old man once

haven't forgotten the world once

still i have missed my whole youth once

i still am a little girl

still dreaming of being like those movie girls

while other girls made their life their movie

while the girls around me are the movie girls

i want to audition and play a role

only a side character

to watch the girls in the movie

only a little closer

not in the last theater row

but here i am

scared, anxious, worried and timid

sobbing every night hasn't brought me anywhere

am still watching from the last row

and i'll never get closer

than buying theater tickets and dvds

because the movie girls are out of my league

and i try to hate them

for the way they live without a second thought

for the way the live my childhood dream

of being like the girls in the movies

but it's not their fault i'm scared to audition

it's not their fault i'm so damn scared

scared of finally living my childhood dream

of being like those girls in the movies

of my life being like a movie

and maybe one day i'll be the main character

of my own movies

-little girl

they say "music on – world off"

but to me the world seems clearer

with a melody filling my ears

shut your eyes

and listen closely

do you hear

the rustling of the leaves

as you wander

through the woods

listen even closer

their steady rustling

sounding like applause

-autumn walk of fame

we still look up to your window

whenever we pass your house

expecting you to sit there

look down on us

and watch from afar

waving and nodding

the way you always did

the way you still do

you still look down on us

and watch us from afar

just from a little further up

-the death of a loved one

on one side

i believe we read

to feel the sadness

other people feel

without experiencing it ourselves

and on the other side

i believe we read

to experience what we feel

through other peoples' words

searching for a mirrored reflection

in another broken soul

just like us, just the way we are

i believe we read

to feel less alone

to feel understood

to feel hugged

with silent tears flowing down

we read to suffer together hand in hand

-backside of my book

i read

to find myself

reflected

in other writers' words

i write to be

somebody else's reflection

it seems as if

a dystopian dream

of fears and tears

became the realest truth

only overnight

years from now

the world shall end

beheaded in fullest force

throat slit up with no mercy

we're dissolving now already

turning into ashes

clouds of dust

until nothing lasts

and one day, maybe soon

they will talk

talk about a former species

called humans

the way we got taught

about the dinosaurs

that ruled the world centuries ago

now buried in ashes

of stones from outer space

except those human kinds

wiped themselves

of the surface of the earth

-the smartest species

what if we

could have put this to an end

before it

needed to be stopped?

dear 2020,

it's crazy to think about how

what's happening is real

that in this here and now

sadness is all we feel

this year held us captive in a dark place

light barely shining through

the sun never reaching our face

i'm not being poetic - it's simply true

tightly gripping metal bars

rattling and trying to fit in between

reaching for the stars

when only clouds are to be seen

this year threw us in a dark cell

all alone, me, myself and i

waiting for the midnight announcing bell

after months of asking when and why

and once the clock strikes twelve

it's over once and for all

we pretend to go back to health and wealth

but for pain new year isn't an unbreakable wall

and once all eyes are shut

you realize new year isn't the desired get-away

it's not a new scene after the cut

it's only 24 hours later, only another day

the date doesn't matter

to know that it's not getting better

-new year, new luck

when life seems pointless

i look outside my window

and i realize

that somehow everything makes sense

at least a little bit

a smile creeps onto my face

looking outside

sunlight peaking out behind the clouds

luring me outside, melting my icy soul

tree branches painting pictures in the sky

making me want to trace them with a pen

the shushing wind running through the fields

shushing the world, shushing every thought

the soft ripple of the surface of the lake

making me want to drown

fresh cool air passing my nostrils

lifting an invisible weight from my chest

blooming flowers dancing in the breeze

dancing through the meadows just like me

bees humming, birds singing

my heart seems to beat in that very rhythm

when life seems pointless

i look outside my window

and remember

how our earth is just existing

for us to destroy her

our beautiful earth

our virtuous earth

careless, dauntless, selfless -

despite it all

our earth exists

the question is how long?

-happy earth day

they don't know that i'm a princess

don't see the sparkling jewels in my crown

don't see me twirling in my gown

don't know because i have never shown

that i'm a princess

because i'm a princess in disguise

they don't know that i'm a princess

i'm not waiting for a strong fearless knight

my palace is nowhere in sight

i'm not sleeping on a pea at night

the way a princess should

because i'm a princess in disguise

-princess me

sometimes i want to be an astronaut

floating through space

not rooted in place

close enough to reach for the stars

no loud noises, no wars, no cars

only silence, nobody but me and i

we think of us humans highly and it is a lie

we say we're the highest form of evolution

all we're capable of is destruction and pollution

sometimes i want to be an astronaut

viewing our earth from far up in space

makes me realize how irrelevant everything is anyways

our existence is so tiny

all we do is being careless and whiny

in the end it doesn't really matter

everything down there - white noise and chitter chatter

all the hate equal as all the love

doesn't matter from above

sometimes i want to be an astronaut

to realize that i'm a blank sheet in the end

no matter how hard i try to bend

nothing but a gathering of particles

not worth any headlines and articles

only existing for a blink of an eye

no purpose, no goal, no reason why

and that makes me feel safe

that makes me feel brave

-in space

not death is our bowser

without walkthrough on the browser

life itself is the final game

a monster not easy to tame

never did i come first in all races

or find all the stars' hidden places

and honestly

i don't want that victory

a win stands for an end

all the highscores turn into sand

and we're back to zero

nothing left of the renowned hero

i am a free bird, i am white

and i do not have the right.

to whine, to complain

because i will never know the caged bird's pain,

because i'm privileged.

white privilege doesn't mean my life's all sickly-sweet honey and only black people get stung by bees,

it's just that my skin colour did not contribute to my life's difficulties.

what i mean is:

if life was a marathon

i would always win,

thanks to the colour of my skin.

if life was a marathon

a black person would never stand a chance

because a black person on the podium doesn't fit into the white man's plans.

a caged bird has no space to spread its wings,

a caged bird is only heard from afar when it sings.

yes, it could test the waters and see how far it's able to go

but as imprisoned bird you do what you have to, not what you want to.

something here is going terribly wrong:

without reason the black community has been the enemy all along.

white folks can't decipher between who's dangerous and who's not.

black folks can't decipher between who's racist and who's not.

people who didn't grow up together

will call each other enemy forever.

it's exposure that is missing -

talking, handshakes, hugging, kissing.

the waters of our society are dirty,

dirty with stereotypes, prejudice and misunderstanding.

sassy, aggressive, overly sexualized -

fearing black citizen is advised.

and stereotypes are like rose coloured glasses -

stereotypes are blinding the masses.

people of colour have been dehumanized.

instead, people of colour have been demonized.

it has taken hundreds if not thousands of lives

to slowly realize

this view is outdated

and there is no way this topic still needs to be debated:

black lives matter just as much as any other life.

now imagine your home is in in flames or about to drown

when calling 911 you'd never say the whole neighbourhood is going down-

so yes, all lives matter

but black lives are aflame.

aflame in the sense of:

american history books teaching white washed fairy tales and fantasy stories

while leaving out black people's lives and worries.

during revolutionary war a long time ago,

not the white wallstreet-wolves and cowboys fought though.

it has always been the black community

who lives out a brutal dehumanizing history.

the world needs to know that it has been the african-americans who have fought

and that's only one reason why african studies need to be taught.

aflame in the sense of:

let's cast one poc per movie for statistics,

to create a colourful racial diversity-mix.

nothing but a sidekick without storyline,

nothing but a stereotyped character design.

the black bestie coming in to save the day,

next to the blonde, white, blue eyed hero using cheap tanning spray.

black people get limited to skin and bones -

as if black people were nothing but copy-paste clones.

nobody dares to look past the colour of skin.

nobody tries to see the unique storylines hidden in plain sight.

only being murdered will get black people on big screens and into the spotlight.

people of colour aren't a new race,

people of colour have always fought for their place.

racism isn't a new word,

racism has always hurt.

but now it's being filmed.

breonna, george, trayvon, michael, tamir -

we know their names around here,

we say their names around here.

yet, we do not want to need to say their names,

we do not want to need to play those 'dead or alive' -games.

there still is no justice, no fairness -

we only hashtag "say their names"

and let twitter burn down in flames.

justice would be hundreds of innocent people still breathing.

and as george floyd so eloquently said "i cannot breathe."

so, justice is something nobody will ever achieve.

childhood and life in general are shaped by society.

key words: police brutality and white supremacy.

racism starts in the womb already,

from the time you're born you live with ptsd.

the racism talk can't wait -

otherwise, it might be too late.

children don't think about colours of skin

children don't know that some colours always loose the marathon and other always win

they don't care until the grownups explain their differences

and how black kids will always have fewer chances

and how black kids will flinch each time the siren rings

until the day they die this triggering sound will shorten their wings.

first lesson: how to act around police men -

also known as how to stay alive

in a world where black people aren't supposed to breathe or vote or even drive.

as a black person one expects to go to jail for crimes one didn't commit

as a black person one can only dream of living in safety and peace for at least a short bit

as a black person one might get murdered in the comfort of their own house.

as a black person one gets used to broken promises and vows.

there have always been moments of protests, blackouts and rooting.

then people fell asleep before one day much later rebooting.

they wake for a momentary uprising and fall asleep again.

it only took dozens of centuries and thousands of dead men,

to finally stand up, to stand hand in hand -

no matter the race.

i am a free bird, i am white

and i do not have the right

to whine, to complain

because i will never know the caged bird's pain

because i'm privileged

i have "white privilege" i can use for good

to support the ones who shed tons of tears and lost gallons of blood

what the world needs isn't another hashtag

what the world needs is for us to have each other's back

the world needs understanding and heart

and one day the black folks are crossing the finish line first and the white people aren't getting a head start

the sewage system is fixed and the waters of our society are clearing,

no emergency calls will be needed to keep houses from searing.

gamechanger -

one day racism won't be a danger.

we're moving towards a bigger vision of liberation

and the first step is sharing information.

we have to start with listening, learning what is going on, supporting -

our voices can bridge the gap of misunderstanding.

hashtag diversity as improvement is now trending.

together we can be the ray of hope the world has been waiting for.

so, let's free the caged birds forever -

sparrow and a mockingbird can sing together

birds belong into the sky.

there's enough space for all birds to fly.

wherever, whenever.

-about birds

"why won't you take off your mask?"

and i really didn't want him to ask

nonetheless i reply

"not until the day i die"

"just take off that damn mask, bro"

and i simply tell him "no

i don't feel like it"

"don't be a kid."

"i'm not."

"then take off the damn thing!"

i look at him – and hear a 'ding'

"you mean that blue cellulosic piece of shit?"

"yes, idiot. glad you noticed."

and only then it hit me

and i wondered how i didn't see

and didn't understand

he meant the (now scrunched up) fabric in my hand

nothing else, nothing more

not the invisible mask i always wore

-masks

FOUR

INTO THE
LIGHT

to me, love poems always felt so sappy

now i realize that all the poet is, is happy

happy, so in love, so full their heart

words just flow naturally, every verse, like you, is art

i never imagined myself to write like this

i didn't know the feeling of your hands, your heart, your love, your kiss

-a first

you're my best friend

she said

and then she kissed me

and made love to me

her fingertips

dancing on my waist

"you are my favorite"

i answer, kissing her harder

smiling into the kiss

since you've come into my life i haven't written all too much

because writing always was my way of coping

and now you're my ink and paper

your ink fills all the pages of my life

not the way my pen does though

because your ink is bright, it's colorful

your ink is red, means love and warmth

your ink is blue, means calmness and safety

your ink is green, means euphoria and hope

you mean happiness

-happily in love

thank you

for saving me

when i was so lost

i didn't even know

i needed to be saved

dancing, screaming through my room

out of happiness, carelessness

but usually, it is out of sadness and frustration

feeling the beaming sun and summer breezes on my skin

no worries, no problems troubling me

but usually even those things trouble me

listening to happy, sappy, preppy songs

and actually relating, humming along

but usually, i go back to sad songs, crying in my room

you make my "usually" a rarely

because you make me dance and scream

because you help me worry less

because you are my happy song

-you are music to my ears

hearing the noises of the random tv show we put on

because we knew the show choice wouldn't matter

wouldn't matter because we wouldn't watch it anyways

too lost in one another, lost in the feeling of you

feeling your hand slowly creeping up my thigh

the already blurry figures on the screen

continuously fading away

already blurry because my mind is everywhere but with them

i am full of you, your soul, your body – intertwined with mine

smelling the bowl of popcorn spilled on the floor

and we didn't care because we turned off the world

our quickening breath and heartbeat and nothing else filling the
silence

only us, only me who knows the feeling of your hands exploring,
touching, finding their place on my skin

tasting your lips, your tongue the dark chocolate and soda covering them

and nothing else, our lips fitting like two puzzle pieces

you're everything i want to taste, maybe forever

and even though your taste is never twice the same it's my favorite

seeing a weak shimmer of flickering light from the tv

but still – the only thing i see is you

even with closed eyes i can see your messy hair and rosy cheeks

read and swollen lips and your half-closed eyelids

all my senses are filled with you, just like all the chapters of my life

-netflix n' chill

it's waking up, getting ready because of an appointment

and coming back to bed

to bathe in your warmth once again

it's getting a shopping cart and comparing prizes

and buying groceries for dinner

because it's like there has always been an us

it's watching an attention craving six-year-old

and cuddling and playing

because it feels like we're a family

it's late nights and youtube and facemasks

and falling asleep with your arms around my waist

and i never want to sleep alone again

it's leaving you and going home

missing you the second your lips leave mine

because you've become my home

it's not a moment or a thought but a feeling

and i know i can see a future, a future with you

-glimpses

every time you leave

a hole inside my chest will stay

a hole shaped like you

my heart is aching

for you to fill the empty space

i didn't even know existed

and every time you leave

a part of me leaves too

i let you take my heart with you

because i am fully yours

love

just existing

every day and everywhere

rooted inside my heart

you

promise me that you'll be my shoulder to cry one?

even though no one knows if one day you'll be gone

promise me that everything will be alright?

even though there is no day without the night

promise me that i'll always get to call you mine?

even though it might not be reality and that's fine

promise me you won't leave me alone?

even though one day you might not be the first person i call on the phone

promise me that you'll stay?

even though you can't promise that you won't go away

promise me that we'll always be together?

even though there is no forever

promise me not to promise me anything at all?

even though it's easier than the truth, easier than the down fall

promise me not to say forever, not to say always?

even though it sounds better than a million "nows" and "todays"

-pinky promise

i was just making myself a sandwich

and i thought

"wouldn't it taste better

if you were with me?"

you're my home

and every minute i fear

my house might burn in flames

what i didn't know was

it has been burning all along

what i didn't know was

that there was nothing left

but ashes

all along

and i'm the phoenix

bathing in your ember

reborn in your flames

because you're home

and you're on fire

setting me aflame

-the phoenix kind of love

i'm always saying sorry

but i'm waiting for the day i won't have to worry

because i'm always saying sorry

because i always worry

about how others feel, what others think

i'm not putting up a fight, not stepping in that rink

it's uncharted territory and who knows

what happens next so i'm the one that bows

i'm always apologizing

even when i didn't do a thing

i just want everyone to be alright

i always just wanted to be somebody's light

i always wanted to be somebody's day after a long night

i always take the blame

i always take the shame

i'm always the one to swallow

the anger, the anxiety, the sorrow

i'm always the one to pretend not to care

about my own right and feelings and share

an apology, a laugh, a hug

but one day i'll decide that i don't give a fuck

it won't matter what everybody thinks

i won't be the one that shrinks

it won't be my fault that my words are misunderstood

and i won't be saying sorry, for good.

-sorry not sorry

we see each other everyday

but when you're gone

all i want you is to stay

and one day – it might get better

your days won't be as sad, the next one even sadder

and one day – you might smile brighter

you won't need to wake up and be a fighter

and one day – you might be simply careless

your life won't be that much of a mess

and one day – you'll look back to all the tears you've shed

and realize that now you're not that sad and life isn't that bad

and one day – you'll leave behind the sorrow

and realize that what matters is only the tomorrow

and one day – you'll know what got you through the night

and it'll be a tiny spark of hope that was your light

and one day – you'll know that hope is the only thing that keeps you alive

-future prognosis

it's not you

i always write about

but it's you who makes me write

in the first place

i realize

my night feels empty without you

in my arms

without your fingertips stroking my hair

your soft lips on mine

not being with you feels so wrong

without seeing your smile

your face not being the last one i see

no good night wishes on our late-night calls

and i realize

my life feels empty without you, too

what would i do

without you?

one morning

when i was waking up my 7-year-old son

he looked me in my eyes

and told me he was sick

that he couldn't go to school

i looked back in his eyes

and i knew that he was lying

he wasn't sick

he just didn't want to go

the fear in his eyes spoke for itself

i made him a tea

and told him to continue sleeping

it was his first mental health day off of school

-mental health day

today i went on a walk

all by myself, nobody but me

as i was wandering around

no schedule to keep, no place to be

through the neighborhood

i've known since the day i was born

almost since forever

my nose was cold, my cheeks stained red

and it was exactly what i needed

i haven't been feeling good about myself today

and i wanted to push those feelings away

so, i went on a walk

for only a few minutes

the facemask hanging on a fence

empty aspirin in the grass

children screaming, birds chirping

the red, round and rich apples in almost every garden

and in ours too

the seemingly infinite fields of corn

that i wanted to steel a cob from

the chestnuts in the crowns and on the floor

but i couldn't find one

i've lived here for years

i walked those roads for over a decade

still, it felt like an adventure

and it was as if i noticed everything

for the very first time

even though i've seen it

a million times

and i still don't feel better about myself

but i am more okay with it now

after i went on a walk

-strolling through the neighborhood

sometimes the past hurts

just as much as the future

but then i hold your hand

and remember

that the present isn't all too bad

all this heartbreak poetry makes me fear

that one day you might not be here

that our finger won't be intertwined no more

emptiness taunting me where you were laying before

left the stinging pain of where your fingers used to rest

the aching hole inside my chest

the warmth of your hands gently grabbing my chin

was if someone sculpted your touch into my skin

the shadow of your being dancing through my mind

because you, my love, were the one i never thought i'd find

now i remember that all i read was poetry

and you are lying next to me

you cuddle closer like you always do

and whisper the words „i love you "

leaning down to kiss the mole on your chin

i love you, too, i want to say, more than you imagine

-heartbreak poetry

tonight, i have to sleep alone

i build myself a mountain chain

made out of squishy pillows

resembling the shape of your body

the softness of your hand

tracing the skin on my waist

your warmth is missing

even your breath on my neck

even though i hate it

good night, baby

i whisper into the darkness

nothing but silence, no answer

but i know you're thinking about me too

-nights alone

you didn't teach me love

how to love

or how to be loved

but you taught me the value of true love

to fight for love

to hold onto it

to nourish and water love

like your favorite ikea plant

i want to call myself a writer

i want to call myself a poet

while struggling to write

no idea is new

no "never been here before"

thousands of romance novels

a million broken hearted idiots

my words - a few in mere millions

it has been thought and felt by others

it has been said before

it has been written down years ago

nothing new

but it has never been thought or felt by me

but it has never been said with my words

it has never been written down by me

i don't use tons of metaphors

i do not compare, no ellipses and symbols

my verses don't flow, my words don't rhyme

my poems aren't the most beautiful

i do not tell the stories from tomorrow

and i still get to call myself a writer

because i tell the stories from today

just like many people did before me

and nobody else's today will ever be mine

nobody's voice will ever be mine

i am a writer, i am a poet

not because of my writing

but because i write

-wannabe writer

where ever i am

whenever i see something beautiful

i want you

to see the same beauty i do

most of all i want you to see

the beauty i see

when looking at you

i want you to see yourself

as just as beautiful

as i think you are

i want you to love yourself

as much as i love you

i'm the girl that wants to be kissed in the rain

and dances in the warm sunlight

the one that stays up until late at night

and needs an early breakfast to stay sane

i'm the girl that dances through her room

while studying

and turns off the tv's sound to synchronize the scenes herself

the one that loves reading and has a dozen of books on her shelf

and a "where is left and right"-kind of being

i'm the girl that loves taking notes

and stammers all the time as soon as she raises her voice

the one that often wants to be alone but needs

and remembers various book and movie quotes

i'm the girl that writes all the day long

and doesn't dare to talk that often

the one whose smile needs to soften

and has been hurt and came out on the other side strong

-that girl

you are my first forever

i see only you and i together

the phrase i always say, those words

thinking you won't be my only forever hurts

and still, i know - i would love for you

to be my last forever too

it's been a year

since our paths intertwined

i fell for you

and i'd always fall again

but more so

i gave myself to you

i gave you my heart

and i never want it back

thanks to you

i found my place in the world

right beside you

in your arms

that's where home is

home is you

and only you

you are my world

the air i breathe

the warmth i feel

you're everything i need

the other half

i didn't know i was looking for

you make me whole, you fill my void

everything clears up

when your eyes meet mine

you keep me sane

make tears turn dry

a year ago, you asked me

to define the word love

today i'd only say your name

you are love

here i am

back in my room

and everything is quiet

when you left

you took all i am, all of me with you

and now my room is empty

the way my bed and desk belong

you are part of this small room

you're my favorite interior design

sometimes i wish we would've met sooner

years ago, already

but then i think again

and everything seems adequate

the way it is right now

our time wasn't years ago it's today

tomorrow

and years from this moment

once upon a time

you weren't the first person

i'd notice walking into the room

i can't grasp the fact

that i didn't see you

the way you glow

brighter than the sun

the way you are the light in every room

the light in the darkness of this world

us, human beings

have always been looking

for something magical

for some bibbidi-bobbidi-boo-kinda shit

yet – we found it long ago

the closest thing we'll ever get

to sparkly stars swirling around

the closest thing we'll ever get

to magic

is the feeling of love

i allow myself to fall

because i know

that you'll be there

to catch me

each and every time

each and every day i fall for you

a little more

-trust falls

thank you, my love

for putting the pieces

back into places

every time i break

when i forget

what i looked like being whole

if you were a map of the world

i'd never get lost

out in the wilderness

because i've explored

you to your bone

my fingers finding their home

raking through your hair

resting on your cheek

you are a map of the world

and i'll never get lost

-my world

i got to meet your family

and you got to meet that family of mine

i introduced you as the person i was dating

now you're more my family

than most people

i grew up with

this has been going on for months, weeks and days
can't think straight anymore anyways.
i can't remember our world the way she used to be
and i wish you, darling, would rescue me
i wish we could pack our things and flee
once and for all and never look back - for good.
but you're not here, you probably don't know
that every time you don't snap back
that every time my memes stay unliked
i feel claustrophobic in my own room,
the walls closing in,
the air getting thin
as if you were holding everything in place
and you do - hold me.
you keep me from getting insane,
you help me cope with the pain,
you prevent me from losing touch with reality,
from losing myself, from losing me.

you're holding me -
not in your arms, not my hand
and really, you're no holding me at all.
you and i, we're not together
forced to be apart, no being together ever
tightly intertwined: arm in arm, hand in hand,
that mundane imagination got banned.
zoom, facetime und skype,
videochatting is our generations' vibe
the new normal, the new now and here
but you know that already.
our new world is strongly characterised by the word distance
don't give up, head's up, smile on your face
because motivational tumblr quotes can actually brighten up the days
to be honest i just want things to go back to how they were before

but what even is normal anymore?
we talk about nothing else all day long
we complain about how everything feels wrong
with that phrase we could write a breakthrough-song
i want things to go back to normality
but nowadays normal is prosperity
and we -
we don't even know what our normal is
we don't remember normalities' bliss.
the normal i didn't cherish and appreciate
my normal didn't matter to me
regarded it as nothing but a matter of course and naturalness
until there was nothing natural left amidst this mess

five feet, hundred kilometres between us two
suddenly everything seems far away
from one to the other day.
where yesterday masses of people danced,
is today everybody socially distanced.
junk food, tiktok, netflix, no place to be.
once upon a time i'll admit
i dreamed of that shit
today i wanna be forced again
to do things, wake up from that nightmare, have a plan
social distancing and loneliness
was in no way my dream.
today, i only want my normal back

and while playing hide and seek with it
i stumbled upon you, unintentionally i'll admit
i slid into your dms on instagram
and the scavenger hunt for normality ended.
now, i want my normal back a little less
maybe the new normal hold luck and happiness.
because without you i'd be lost
because when i can't find the light switch in the dark
when it hurts, costs effort to get out of bed
and even my ikea plants hang their head -
then you're here to pick me up

to catch me when i fall
you light up candles and lighten up the way
a shoulder to cry on, open ear at any time of the day
virtually tightly embraced
you're here, you're listening.
you give me strength, you radiate light
and make me believe that somehow some time everything will be
alright
but you probably don't even know
how much i really need you.
i mean how could you?
between us is always this taunting distance
merely as separating as a fence.
nothing can separate us two,
nothing can separate our hearts too.
this sounds like a romantic sunday- evening blockbuster to me
but i'm not talking about the new cheesy nicholas sparks lovestory.
sorry, not sorry,
this is not a lovestory
and there's no happy-end
still - i'm talking about loving
the things that last - love lasts
the things that stay - hope stays
the things that stick around –
you stick around
despite the distance

it's been a year in solitary confinement
call it however you want - maybe also imprisonment
if i had known what was there to come
i'd hugged you tighter
i would have smiled brighter
and looking back it's pretty sad
that only after weeks of laying in my bed
staring at the ceilings without end
i realised that other people are a heaven-sent

i've learned to cherish every human being accompanying me
instead of replacing them with indoor greenery
i've learned to cherish my mates -
instead of cancelling countless dates
i've learned that some things end too fast
and that we waste our time way too often at last
the wireless vibe, you probably remember:
the deep instagram-snapchat-tiktok-hole
no other way to stay in touch
the only way to get time to pass by
and the worlds' still turning
and despite the mourning
the end is far away, not yet in sight
but i'm always accompanied by a light
a light, that's us, that's you, that's me
today - distance between us, we share the same destiny
stronger connected than in the years before
connected despite the distance and the masks we wore

-relatively far away

weather changes

clouds pass by

sun will push through

grey will turn blue

or at least bluish

bluish with a tinge of hope

ACKKNOWLEDGEMENT AND ABOUT THE AUTHOR

thank you.

thank you, mum

for how you imagine walking into a bookstore

with my published bestseller work

before i published anything at all.

thank you, grany

for promising to read my poetry

with google translate

because you don't speak english.

thank you, sylvana

for subtly promoting my book

and reading it yourself

despite the fact that you never read.

thank you, emma

for creating art with me

and helping me design the cover

even though you don't draw flowers usually.

thank you, yes…you

for buying and reading my book

because to you this is just one book among many

and you have no idea how much it means to me.

hey.

i'm magnolia d. reeves.

i'm seventeen.

i'm german.

i haven't even graduated yet.

i have no idea where life will take me.

but I know writing has been my passion

for as long as i can remember.

this is the first time

i'm brave enough to publish something.

life hasn't always been easy for me

and I know neither has it for you

but now

we can suffer together

hand in hand.